THE *Little Book* OF

~

HERBS

~

**A FASCINATING LOOK AT THE
AROMATIC WORLD OF HERBS**

DEDICATION:
For my mother

Disclaimer
Care should be taken when using herbs.
Some may cause an allergic reaction.
Neither the author nor the publisher can be
held responsible for any adverse reactions to the
herbs, recipes or formulas discussed within.

Editor: Fleur Robertson
Editorial Assistance: Kirsty Wheeler
Original Design Concept: Peter Bridgewater
Design: Stonecastle Graphics Ltd
Director of Production: Gerald Hughes
Production: Ruth Arthur, Sally Connolly, Neil Randles
Typesetting: Julie Smith

Published by
CHARTWELL BOOKS, INC.
A Division of **BOOK SALES, INC**.
110 Enterprise Avenue
Secaucus, New Jersey 07094
CLB 3146
© 1993 CLB Publishing Ltd
Godalming, Surrey, England.
Printed and bound in Singapore.
All rights reserved.
ISBN 1 55521 988 8

THE *Little Book* OF
HERBS

MARGARET CARTER

CHARTWELL
BOOKS, INC.

What is a Herb?

What is a herb? One definition states that any plant of use to man can be called a herb. Certainly our ancestors relied on more than simply the little patch of herbs beside the kitchen door. They depended on a wide range of plants to add zest to their meals, for medicines and cosmetics, to scent their linen and to sweeten the air – and even to allow them to see the fairies or revive a lover's waning interest! Thus a plant useful in any of these ways was considered a herb. Over the years, as many of these herb uses have fallen from favor, been replaced by modern equivalents or just forgotten, the herb garden itself has shrunk. Some of the plants once considered herbs are now in the flower garden, some have been redefined as wild flowers, and others are seen as mere weeds! Magic potions may be a thing of the past, but the recent revival of interest in all other things herbal might yet see the return of old favorites to their former status in the herb garden.

Formal Herbs

In medieval Europe, the cultivation of herbs was the province of monks. They made beautiful copies of existing texts on the uses of herbs and then extended their knowledge through first-hand experience of the herbs they grew.

With the invention of printing, information about herbs reached a wider audience and interest in growing them spread. People began to plant their own herb gardens.

Knot gardens were a particularly popular development of the 1600s. Laid out near the house, the knot garden was a formal geometric design outlined in one kind of plant – evergreen box was a favorite – and filled with a patchwork of various herbs. A few such herb gardens are still cultivated in Europe and America today.

Herbs in Homes of the Past

In past ages, every householder would have grown a variety of herbs for domestic purposes, and each family would have kept treasured herb recipes. Sage, for example, was eaten for its health-giving properties, as well as being used as an antiseptic, an astringent and for strewing over the floor to disguise unpleasant household smells.

Historically, herbs were grown for two specific culinary reasons. Firstly, they were used to disguise both the lack of variety in people's diets and the blandness of many foodstuffs. They were used to hide any lack of freshness, for people could rarely afford to throw food away, particularly in the barren winter months.

Secondly, herbs were included in the diet for medicinal purposes. The old herbalists had a holistic view of health: they believed that good health was not simply the absence of illness, but involved the positive maintenance of well-being. So herbs were used not only to cure an ailment, but also to keep the body fit and well.

12

Preserving Herbs

Herbs are best harvested before they flower, when their flavor is strongest. On a dry day, pick the herbs after the dew has gone, but before the sun has dispersed their essential oils.

The two main methods of preserving herbs are freezing and drying. To freeze, either put sprigs of the individual herbs into bags and pop these into the freezer, or chop them and freeze them with an equal amount of water in ice-cube trays. In both cases, the herbs can be used directly from frozen.

To dry herbs, tie them in bunches and hang these upside down in a warm, dry place: the airing cupboard is ideal. Drying times will vary: the herbs should be left until they are crisp, but not powdery. The dried herbs should be stored in dark, airtight jars and kept in a cool place out of direct light. In these conditions, they will keep their flavor for about six months.

The Herb Garden

The atmosphere of a herb garden is one of peace and restfulness, a sunny sanctuary, drowsy with heady scents and the gentle hum of insects. Add their usefulness to this aesthetic appeal, and who could resist finding the space to grow their own herbs?

Herbs may be grown as a decorative edging to vegetable plots: this works particularly well for herbs such as parsley which need to be grown in large quantities to satisfy the cook's needs. The more colorful or architectural varieties of herbs, such as purple sage or bronze fennel, fit well into modern flower borders. Alternatively, positioning herbs where their fragrance can be fully enjoyed makes good sense; planting a

rosemary bush by the garden path, for instance, means that it will perfume the air every time someone brushes past.

Where herbs are to have their own plot, it is best to site this near the kitchen. If herbs are grown together in this way, the untidy nature of many species means they often look most attractive planted informally within a more formal framework. This does not entail great labor. For example, a certain formality of setting can be achieved by planting herbs between paving stones to brighten a patio. Raised beds also provide a convenient framework for a small herb garden, and take some of the backstrain out of maintenance and picking.

Potted Herbs

Lack of space should not prevent anybody from enjoying the benefits of fresh herbs. A collection of pots planted with several culinary species makes a decorative and productive addition to any patio, backyard, or balcony. Where space is really limited, a strawberry planter can be planted up to form a mini herb garden. Even a sunny window can be put to use, either to host a herb-planted window box on the ledge outside, or to provide light and warmth for shelves of potted herbs indoors. A light, warm spot inside is also a good place to keep tender herbs over the winter. Herbs with invasive tendencies, such as mint, are well suited to being grown in pots, as are herbs, such as basil, that are attractive to slugs.

Never allow herbs to dry out during the growing season and fertilize them regularly. Repot once a year in the spring or, if this is not possible, renew the top two inches of compost.

18

Herbal Lore

Old books on herbs contain a heady mixture of fact, superstition and magic that still fascinates and entertains. However, some of the herbal lore they recorded is actually being vindicated by modern research. To take one example, feverfew's ancient reputation for curing headaches and giddiness is currently being upheld by scientists, whose research indicates the herb can provide relief for migraine sufferers.

Other traditions demonstrate the lighter side of ancient lore. In classical times, borage taken in wine was thought to promote joyousness, though sceptics might argue as to the true source of the merriment. Yet the tradition is continued at many social gatherings, especially in England, where the alcoholic fruit cup known as Pimm's is still decorated with borage leaves and flowers.

On a more practical level, garlic is still planted near rose bushes by countrymen because of its reputation for chasing away greenfly who dislike its scent. As an old and "green" tradition, it is worth trying today, though admittedly, the aesthetic appeal of the garlic plant is limited.

Basil

Sweet basil (*Ocimum basilicum*) is a herb of contradictions, and an inspirer of arguments, which manages to symbolize both love and hate. Thus some cultures connected basil with the devil, while others respected the herb for its reputed power against witches.

Sweet basil is actually a native of India, where it is sacred to the Hindus, who believe that the herb should only be picked if worthy use is to be made of it. Although not considered sacred in Europe, the plant's name is derived from the Greek word for royal, suggesting that basil was a herb thought fit for a king. There is, however, nothing regal in the tradition of

sowing the herb with an oath or a curse, a tradition that is reflected in the French expression *semer le basilic* (literally "to sow basil") meaning to slander. The old herbalists claimed basil and rue would not grow together, although this may just reflect the incompatibility of their two distinctive aromas.

Famous in Mediterranean cookery, basil's strong flavor does not appeal to everyone, though it's essential in Italian cooking. It teams well with tomatoes, but its best-known culinary contribution is to the classic Genovese dish, pesto, a sumptuous sauce that transforms pasta into a dish that is truly fit for a king.

Bay

The sweet bay (*Laurus nobilis*) is an evergreen native of the Mediterranean region, where it was once sacred to Apollo, the sun god. As the true laurel plant, it is the leaves of the bay which were woven into wreaths by the ancient Greeks and used to crown both victors in battle and distinguished poets. It is thanks to this custom that we still speak of winning our laurels.

In sixteenth-century England it was held that bay leaves should be burnt to cleanse the air of plague germs. The herb was also regarded as providing protection against the devil, to which end Nicholas Culpeper advised, "... neither witch nor devil, thunder nor lightning will hurt a man where a bay tree is."

Yet it is as a culinary herb that sweet bay is best known and it has a multitude of uses in savory dishes. One leaf is usually enough to flavor a dish, but woe betide the cook who forgets to remove it, for the leaves are impossible to eat. A bay leaf is essential to a bouquet garni,

24

a basic in French cuisine. Infusing a leaf in hot milk before using it to make a bechamel sauce greatly enhances the sauce's flavor.

The bay makes a fine specimen plant in a tub, and can be clipped into neat, formal shapes, as it was in gardens of old. The plant needs a sheltered, sunny spot and should be moved under cover in winter, for it is not totally hardy.

Garlic

Garlic (*Allium sativum*) has been reviled throughout history for its side effects; as far back as ancient Egyptian times it was thought to be fit only for the lower classes, whose stomachs were tough enough to cope! However, it was known to have positive qualities too. As well as being respected for its power to ward off infection, garlic has long been used as an antiseptic: French soldiers cleansed their wounds with garlic in the First World War.

Many of garlic's powers are linked with its "repellent" properties; movie-goers everywhere know of the herb's effect on vampires, and once garlic was carried to render witches powerless. More practically, the sixteenth-century herbalist Gerard was confident that placing garlic in a mole's run would make it leave immediately.

In the Middle Ages, it was held that the curative properties of a herb could be deduced from its appearance. As the hollow leaves of the garlic plant most resembled the windpipe, it was used to cure diseases of that part of the body, and is still recommended for bronchitis and other respiratory complaints.

On the culinary side, garlic fans claim most savory dishes are better for its addition, and even sceptics are being won over to their view.

Lavender

The scent of lavender (*Lavandula officinalis*) was once prized not just for cosmetic purposes, but also for its relaxing properties and for the positive effect it was held to have on the brain. Harvesters often wore a sprig of lavender under their hats to fend off the head colds and headaches that prevented them working at that busy time.

Lavender, though a native of sunny Mediterranean hillsides, is thought of as an English plant. Probably introduced into England by homesick Romans, the plant was later grown commercially, a tradition that continues today.

The clean smell of lavender has always been one of its main attributes; the Romans scented their washing water with the herb, which derives its name from the Latin verb *lavare*, meaning to wash. Lavender has been used ever since in cosmetics, perfumes, and scented sachets. Less familiar is its use as a culinary herb. Once used in sweet dishes, today it can be found in desserts, and in jellies accompanying rich meat.

Sweet Marjoram

Native to central Europe, sweet marjoram (*Origanum majorana*) is said to have been grown by Venus. The herb has many connections with happiness, its botanical name being two ancient Greek words meaning "joy of the mountain." The Greeks held that if marjoram grew on a person's tomb it meant they were happy, while the herbalist Gerard recommended marjoram tea for people "given to overmuch sighing."

Marjoram's fragrance made it a very popular herb for domestic uses, particularly for scattering on the floor to cover up bad household smells. The herb was also sewn in linen bags for cupboards, for it not only scented the contents but also repelled insects, especially moths. The leafy tops of the plant were added to furniture polish and herb pillows.

30

Mint

Mint, as any gardener will tell you, is invasive, though this is usually forgiven it because of its culinary usefulness. Legend claims that the herb takes its name from the nymph Minthe, who, loved by Pluto, the god of the underworld, was changed into the plant by his jealous wife.

The famous combination of roast lamb and mint sauce may be more than just fortuitous, since mint actually cuts through the fattiness of meats such as lamb and helps them to be digested. This may in turn explain the modern enjoyment of the after-dinner mint, and suggests why peppermint tea is used for indigestion.

Usually used in sauces and jellies for eating with meat, mint also makes a fine flavoring for cream or cottage cheeses and, of course, it is also an essential ingredient of that most evocative of summery drinks, the mint julep!

33

Parsley

Parsley (*Petroselinum crispum*) is a king among herbs. In Greek mythology, it sprang from the spilt blood of the hero Archemorus, and was ever after venerated and used to crown champions at the Isthmian Games. The *Grete Herbal* of 1526 suggests that curly-leaved parsley is obtained by stamping on the seeds to bruise them before planting. Bruised or not, its seeds germinate very slowly, supposedly because they must go to the Devil and back seven times before germinating! Impatient gardeners can water in the seeds with boiling water to speed things up.

Parsley's uses in savory dishes are countless: it is an essential ingredient of such classics as bouquet garni, fines herbes and maître d'hôtel butter. Cooks might like to surprise friends by serving deep-fried parsley: unusual and delicious.

Rosemary

Rosemary (*Rosmarinus officinalis*) is a native of the shores of the Mediterranean, and its name means "dew of the sea." Well known to symbolize remembrance, it was linked with funerals, yet it was also carried at weddings to symbolize fidelity.

The growth of the plant has several religious associations. One tradition says that its lifespan is equal to the thirty-three years that Jesus lived on earth. Another tradition claims that once the plant has attained the height of Christ it will only increase in breadth. It was also commonly held that rosemary would only thrive in the gardens of the righteous. On a more worldly note, an old saying claims that "where rosemary flourishes, the woman rules." Indeed, in general the old herb books rejoice in the subject of rosemary, including this delightful piece of advice: "boil the leaves in white wine and wash thy face therewith and thy brows and thou shalt have a fair face."

Rosemary is best used on its own in cooking because of its overpowering flavor. It marries particularly well with lamb, but also enhances the flavor of other roast meats.

Sage

The health-giving properties of sage (*Salvia officinalis*) were highly thought of in past ages; the plant's name is derived from the Latin verb "salvere," meaning to save or to heal and it was once regarded as something of a cure-all. "How can a man die when there is sage in his garden?" runs an old Arab proverb, and sage's association with immortality descends through the centuries to emerge in England as: "He that would live for aye, Must eat sage in May." Although specifying the month might seem fussy, it is true that the herb's flavor is at its very best just before it flowers in early summer.

If eating sage could guarantee a person's future, the herb could also help them see into it. Any intrepid young woman wishing to know in advance the identity of her husband had supposedly only to pick twelve sage leaves at midnight on Hallowe'en to see his shadowy figure approach.

Sage is particularly associated with pork, but will combine equally well with other meats, such as duck or goose, as the oil in the leaves cuts through their fattiness. The herb's strong taste means that it is best used on its own, and sparingly, or it will overwhelm other flavors.

Thyme

A Mediterranean native, thyme (*Thymus*) was highly esteemed by both the Romans, who thought it cured melancholy, and the ancient Greeks, who regarded it as an emblem of courage. This latter association continued into the Middle Ages, when ladies would present a sprig of thyme to their knights to inspire them with the necessary courage for jousts and battles. Alternatively, a knight's lady might embroider a thyme sprig with a bee onto a scarf, which could also impart courage to the wearer. Bees and thyme were an apt combination, for the one is greatly attracted to the other, and the honey produced by bees that feed on thyme is particularly flavorsome.

As ornamental garden plants, varieties of the creeping thyme (*Thymus serpyllum*) look very attractive when planted between paving stones to soften the hard lines of terraces and patios. In cooking, thyme is delicious sprinkled on meats at a barbecue, and is also good in summer salads.

Basil Salad

To make this lovely Italian salad is simplicity itself – the trick lies in attractive presentation.

2 avocados
Lemon juice
2 beef tomatoes
8oz/225g mozzarella cheese
A handful of fresh basil
6 tbsps French dressing

Halve the avocados, remove the stones, peel and cut into slices. Sprinkle the slices with lemon juice to prevent them discoloring. Slice the tomatoes and the mossarella cheese thinly and arrange the salad ingredients attractively on four plates. Chop most of the basil, stir it into the dressing and spoon it over the salad. Decorate with the remaining fresh basil leaves.

Herb Butters and Cheeses

Gifts of home-made foods are always much appreciated by gourmet friends, and what could be tastier than a variety of butters and cheeses flavored with fresh herbs from the garden? A selection packed into a little basket, and decorated with a few sprigs of fresh herbs tied into a bouquet garni, makes a perfect present.

A rough guide for herb butter is to add two tablespoons of chopped herbs to every ounce. The possibilities are endless, but a few classic combinations are: maître d'hôtel butter, flavored with parsley, lemon juice and a pinch of cayenne pepper (great melted over steaks or vegetables); tarragon butter, perfect for chicken dishes; and

dill butter, which is wonderful with fish. Pack the butters into ramekins and cover with discs of waxed paper. Use as soon as possible.

Adding herbs to shop-bought curd or cream cheese is a quick and easy gift idea. Minced garlic makes a pungent addition, while mint, parsley, chives or dill transform plain cheeses. Either mix the chopped herbs or garlic thoroughly into the cheese before packing the mixture into ramekins, or roll the cheese into shapes, coat these with chopped herbs (not garlic), and wrap them in waxed paper. As a rule, one tablespoon of herbs or one clove of minced garlic to every eight ounces/225g of cheese is about right.

Herb Preserves

No-one can resist the appeal of a kitchen shelf glowing with jars of home-made preserves. Made as other preserves, jams and jellies aromatized with fresh herbs make very welcome gifts.

Herb jellies often have an apple base; mint is the classic flavoring, but rosemary, sage or thyme are also used. If old-fashioned roses are in the herb garden, make delicious rose-petal jam – a real taste of yesteryear. Pot the preserves in attractive jars, and, if they are gifts, top them with fabric, perhaps edged with lace, and tie this with ribbons or raffia. Add a herb sprig to finish.

Mint and Onion Chutney

2 tbsps olive oil
1 large onion, coarsely chopped
¼ cup fresh mint
1 fresh green chilli pepper, seeded
1 tbsp lemon juice
½ tsp salt, or to taste

Heat the oil over a medium heat, and fry the onion until it is soft, but not brown. Allow to cool. Put the onion and the rest of the ingredients in a processor and blend until smooth. Pack the chutney into a moisture-free, airtight container and refrigerate. It will last for up to four weeks. Served with all types of snacks or an Indian meal, it is an ideal gift for a hot and spicy food addict.

Herb Oils and Vinegars

Keen cooks are always happy to receive new spurs to their creativity. Inspire them to fresh culinary heights with presents of flavored oils and vinegars, which can be used in marinades, salad dressings, casseroles and fondues.

Herbs for oils and vinegars should be picked before they flower, on a dry morning before the sun has evaporated all their flavorsome oils. White wine vinegar and olive oil make the best carriers. In vinegar, tarragon is the most common flavoring, but dill and marjoram are also good. Oils taste best with rosemary, basil, marjoram or thyme. Place a sprig or two of the chosen herb in a sterilized bottle, fill with either vinegar or oil and stopper firmly. Leave for up to a month before use to develop the flavor fully.

Another gourmet gift can be made by rolling goats' cheeses in chopped herbs. These are packed into a storage jar with sprigs of fresh herbs and maybe a peeled clove or two of garlic. The jar is then filled with olive oil and sealed. The cheeses should be allowed to marinate in the oil and herbs for a while before using, so the flavors can develop: the result is truly scrumptious!

Scented Herb Sachets

What could be more delightful than a gift of sweet-smelling sachets made to add their summery fragrance to clothes and linen all winter long? Easy to make from home-dried or shop-bought herbs, they bring a little touch of scented luxury to the home.

Muslin, voile or net are the best fabrics to use for making sachets. Flat sachets for drawers or airing cupboards can be sewn in any shape. Sachets for hanging in wardrobes are easily made from a circle of fabric, which is gathered up round the filling and then tied with ribbon, leaving a loop for hanging. Both types can be trimmed with lace or ribbon, while embroidering the recipient's initials or a herbal motif onto flat sachets makes them very special. For the filling use lavender – a favorite herbal pot pourri mixture – or rosemary, thyme and southernwood: the latter will act as a fragrant moth repellent.

Pillows of sweet-smelling herbs for relaxation make thoughtful gifts for any busy person needing to unwind. Cotton fabric is the best covering. Sew the herbs into a sachet first and place this between the layers of wadding that are the stuffing for the pillow so the herbs can easily be renewed when they begin to lose their potency. Any mix of rosemary, chamomile, lavender, marjoram, lemon verbena and thyme will both soothe and revive jangled nerves.

Herb Bath Gifts

Muslin bath bags, once often used to scent baths, are a lovely tradition worth reviving. Fill them with dried herbs, tie with ribbon and drop them in a full bath or hang them from the tap while it is running. A box of different colored bags containing two mixtures, one relaxing and one reviving, makes a fine gift. Peppermint, rosemary, thyme, and lemon balm are the reviving herbs, while a mixture of chamomile, lavender and rose petals is relaxing. The French beauty Madame de Pompadour used mint, lavender, thyme, rosemary and houseleek in her bath. Less the houseleek, a "Pompadour" mix would be a real historical gift!

Herbal hair rinses – chamomile for blondes and rosemary for brunettes – also make good gifts. Make a strong infusion by boiling sprigs of either herb in sufficient water to cover for fifteen minutes. Strain the mixture into a pretty bottle and top up with still mineral water.

Herb Pot Pourri

1 cup lemon verbena leaves
1 cup chamomile flowers
1 cup mint leaves
1 cup lemon balm leaves
1 cup marigold petals
A little dried lemon peel, crumbled
4 tsps powdered orris root
6 drops lemon oil

Use a large, lidded container. Mix all the ingredients together, seal the container, and put it in the airing cupboard. Leave for about six weeks, giving it a shake every three or four days to allow the mixture to "cure." Add a few colorful dried flowers or fruits to enhance the appearance of the pot pourri on display. As its scent fades, the pot pourri can be revived by adding more drops of lemon oil and extra powdered orris root, mixing them in thoroughly.

Herb Wreath

Using fresh and dried culinary herbs to make a wreath will give a keen cook the practical benefit of the herbs and the joy of a charming kitchen decoration. Using dried as well as fresh herbs will prolong the wreath's useful life, and adding a few spices gives it extra zest.

Buy a wreath base of a suitable size – probably no big than seven inches in diameter – and use thin wire to attach little bunches of bay leaves, rosemary, sage, thyme, parsley, etc. to this. Include a few dramatic seedheads, such as fennel or dill, if available, together with cinnamon sticks, star anise or bulbs of garlic. Distribute the herbs and spices evenly and attractively around the wreath, keeping the arrangement in proportion to the size of the base. If the wreath is to be hung, provide a loop in ribbon, plaited raffia – or even string, for a really rustic look.

The Language of Herbs

Rose *love*
Rosemary *remembrance*
Elderflower *compassion*
Sorrel *affection*
Horehound *health*
Marjoram *happiness*

Fragrant nosegays, known as tussie mussies, were carried in the 1600s to ward off infection. As the danger of plague passed, tussie mussies became symbolic: by the Victorian era they were a way of sending a discreet message. Today using the language of herbs to make gift posies can be great fun. Place the herbs so the central one is also central to the message, wrap them in silk or lace and tie them with ribbon. Add a note on the language of herbs so the recipients can read the message for themselves.

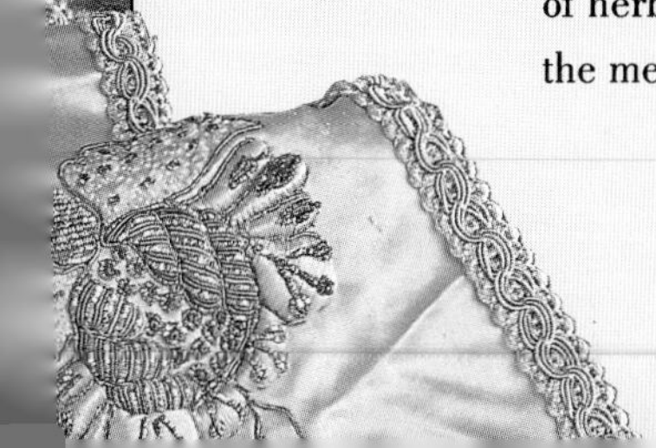

Herb Tales

Hundreds of delightful superstitions, legends and old wives' tales have become attached to herbs over their long and eventful history. Some of these concern domestic harmony. For instance, if periwinkle were eaten in a salad by both husband and wife, it was reputed to inspire mutual love, though some herbalists were sceptical even then. The presence of the pot herb rampion was thought to cause children to quarrel; removing it would solve the problem.

Other tales relate that placing rosemary leaves under a mattress will prevent the sleeper having nightmares; and those planning a long walk might like to follow William Coles' advice from his book *The Art of Simpling* (1656): "If a footman

take mugwort and put it into his shoes in the morning, he may go forty miles before noon and not be weary." Those seeking a cure for baldness could always try sprinkling parsley seeds over their head for three nights in every year, as one old herb book suggests!

On the supernatural side, wearing a piece of angelica root round the neck was reputed to render witches harmless. Less fearsomely, thyme could be used in several recipes that enabled the user to see fairies. In Scandinavian mythology, nettles were sacred to Thor, the god of thunder. During a thunderstorm, people threw nettles onto their fires in the belief that Thor would then prevent their houses being struck by lightning.

$\mathcal{A}$cknowledgements

The publishers would like to thank the following for permission to reproduce:

A-Z BOTANICAL COLLECTION, Hatfield, for pp. 36-37.

THE BRIDGEMAN ART LIBRARY, London, for *Spring*/Valkenborch, pp. 20-21.

E. T. ARCHIVE, London, for pp. 59-59 (insets).

THE GARDEN PICTURE LIBRARY, London, for facing page/title page (Linda Burgess); pp. 10-11 (Clive Boursnell); pp. 14-15 (Mayer/Le Scanff); pp. 18-19; p. 26 (Linda Burgess), pp. 26-27 (Brigitte Thomas); pp. 28-29 (Linda Burgess); p. 31 (inset Marijke Heuff); p. 32 (Mayer/Le Scanff); p. 33 (Clive Nicholls); p. 35 (Vaughan Fleming); p. 38 (Mayer/Le Scanff); pp. 38-39 (Brian Carter); p. 41 (inset David Askham); p. 49 (Mayer/Le Scanff); p. 50 (Gary Rogers).

JOHN GLOVER for pp. 8-9 (main photograph); pp. 16-17; p. 30 (margin); pp. 30-31 (background); pp. 34-35 (background); p. 41 (background).

HARRY SMITH COLLECTION, Chelmsford, for pp. 24-25.

PICTUREPOINT, Windsor, for back flap; p. 22; p. 27.